SLICE OF LIFE
WORSHIP DRAMAS
(VOLUME 1)

SLICE OF LIFE WORSHIP DRAMAS

(VOLUME 1)

Shelly Barsuhn

ABINGDON PRESS
Nashville

SLICE OF LIFE WORSHIP DRAMAS (VOLUME 1)

Copyright © 2007 Rochelle Barsuhn

All rights reserved.

This book is printed on acid-free paper.

Library of Congress Cataloging-in-Publication Data

Nielsen Barsuhn, Rochelle, 1958-
 Slice of life worship dramas / Shelly Barsuhn.
  p. cm.
 ISBN 978-0-687-64325-7 (volume 1) — ISBN 978-0-687-64335-6 (volume 2)
 1. Drama in public worship. 2. Christian drama, American. I. Title.

 BV289.N54 2007
 246'.72—dc22

                                                                    2007004710

07 08 09 10 11 12 13 14 15 16—10 09 08 07 06 05 04 03 02 01

MANUFACTURED IN THE UNITED STATES OF AMERICA

For Scott,
brainstormer, constructive critic, willing servant, and soul mate
and for Sophia and Sam,
beloved children and fellow fans of drama

ACKNOWLEDGMENTS

Many people informed the compilation and writing of this book.

LEITH ANDERSON, senior pastor, first proposed the idea of drama at Wooddale Church nearly two decades ago, and has unwaveringly supported it through its growth pangs and maturation. His standards of excellence make all of us in the drama ministry better at what we do.

BOB JENKINS, most excellent director of drama, always sees more in a script than I put in. His insight, experience, and humor breathe life into the presentations. I don't know a harder worker who makes it all look easy.

DAN COLLISON, worship arts pastor, has a rare and passionate vision for the arts in worship. He's an idea man who always has his finger on the pulse of new ideas and has a gift for pulling diverse artists together.

TO MY MANY ACTOR FRIENDS: Thank you, with admiration. Your abilities humble me and remind me that I am a tiny cog in this ministry. Thank you for your gifts and your dedication to God's work. Writing for you is a privilege.

The Wooddale drama ministry is indebted to the gifted production designers, prop builders, lighting technicians, costume designers, makeup artists, musicians, and many others who get both the big and small presentations off the ground. I fully understand that this ministry could not function without you. You make it all look good and *work*.

SPECIAL THANKS TO THE ACTORS WHO APPEAR ON THE DVD: Nikki Allen, Jerry Barnaby, Kris Barnaby, Scott Barsuhn, Jim Belich, Kelly Belich, Barcy Bergstrom, Kelsey Bohleen, Peter Boyer, Susan Coe, Debbie Erickson, Jessi Fredrickson, Gary Flakne, Delrae Knutson, Chris Maresca, Jennifer Rauen, Jean Rohn, Grant Spickelmier, Ben Tupman, Lisa Walker, Marilyn Williams

The Power of the "Slice of Life" Drama

I love a good story, and there is something especially powerful about true-to-life stories. I don't mean, necessarily, factual stories (biographies and autobiographies, which have their own importance in my library). I mean imaginative literature and stories that are real because they mirror our lives and have something to say about us.

Slice of life dramas are meant to feel authentic. They are short, which limits the time for meaningful character or plot development. But they give a quick picture of the issues or anxieties that real people face. Some slice of life dramas can surprise, touch, or soothe us. They can remind us of the things we humans lack. They can remind us of our need for God's grace.

Contents

Contents

Igniting a Drama Ministry

*I*gniting a Drama Ministry is a grand title with which to begin. Perhaps something more modest is in order, something like *Sparking a Drama Ministry*. Most ministries aren't sudden, roaring fires. Even ministries led by passionate, creative people take time to grow in intensity and heat. Are you ready to nurture a small flame? Ask yourself:

Why Our Church?

Consider the reasons you have for wanting to add or grow a drama ministry in your church. Good reasons include:

- We want to add still more depth to our worship services.
- We want to apply the messages in a personal way.
- Our congregation is ready for drama.
- Our leadership, including the pastor, strongly supports the idea.
- We have individuals who have exceptional talent and drive.
- Our actors don't want glory for themselves or a showcase for their talents. They want to honor God.
- Our volunteers are in this for the long haul.
- We have prayed and believe that this will be a beneficial addition to our services.

Reasons that are not good include:

- Big churches include drama in their services.
- We know a really good actor.
- We want to entertain people.
- We like dramas that express "the moral of the story" for people who might not have caught it from the sermon.

Why Drama?

Not long ago, the arts in evangelical Christian worship were pretty much limited to music. Drama was part of a long-past tradition that got lost somewhere in history. Services featured choirs, pianos, organs, soloists, and musicians, but not actors. Churches were often wary of people gifted in dramatic arts. A volunteer (often feeling stiff and nervous) might stand at the podium or pulpit and read Scripture, or the pastor might recite a few lines of poetry. But people shivered when they thought of inviting actors onto the stage unless it was for the occasional children's Christmas pageant.

Many elements may have contributed to this discomfort. Pastors have had a justifiable fear of worship turning into performance. Or they have had a mortal dread of bad drama. (There is nothing worse than having to suffer through a poorly prepared or badly acted "skit.") And adding drama to services required advance planning and communication by the pastor, who was already stretched thin by responsibilities.

But the early modern practitioners of drama in worship quickly learned that there is much to be gained. Worship that mixes a variety of art—music, Scripture recitation, video, drama, movement—feels fuller and richer. God is honored when individuals use the gifts with which they have been wisely provided. The arts can underscore the week's theme. Sometimes they eloquently express the inexpressible. Not everyone learns or experiences worship in the same way, so using a mixture of the arts can help people *of all kinds* find a connection point.

What is the appeal of drama? It's storytelling. Stories are about people, and we learn through stories. Jesus knew that. Drama can disarm people and make them pause to think. It can prime the pump for information to follow. It can ask questions that listeners need to ask themselves. It can touch nerves. It can commiserate. It can challenge.

Getting Started

Involve Your Pastor

The support and involvement of your senior pastor is the lifeblood of a thriving drama ministry. With the security of his or her enthusiasm, you are free to fly, or at least to test your wings. Your team will feel loved and, therefore, empowered. To be frank, sometimes the affection of your pastor is all you have in the beginning.

Start by asking your senior pastor for a synopsis of the coming year's sermons. When his or her heart pumps with alarm, explain that you don't really need much—just the date, the general topic, a few lines of description, and maybe a Scripture reference or two. Offer any incentive you can devise for your pastor to supply this information, for it is the starting point of your team's creative process. Help your pastor understand that only with advance planning can the drama team prepare well-executed vignettes that augment worship. Let your pastor know that you want to produce dramas that tie in smoothly with the sermon. Remind him or her of the horror of badly done drama that results from a lack of advance planning.

If obtaining a year's worth of topics is impossible, ask for six months or four months. What you're after is adequate time for planning, gathering scripts, casting, propping, and rehearsing. (See the proposed timeline on page 22.)

Early in the process, develop a system of communication with your pastor—meetings or phone calls once per week, per month, per quarter, or whatever meets his or her comfort level. Designate one primary contact (probably the drama director) to serve as the liaison with the pastor. Don't overwhelm your pastor with details, issues, problems, and complaints. He or she needn't—and shouldn't—oversee the day-to-day operations of the ministry but *should* feel included in plans so there are no surprises on the day of performance.

Build Your Team

Fill key positions by approaching people you know rather than by placing notices in the church newsletter or website. (The exception would be periodically announcing an audition for new actors.) By tapping folks whom you trust and who have the skills you seek, you'll save yourself some of the embarrassment of having politely to decline offers of assistance from people who *want* to be involved but lack the necessary skills. This uncomfortable situation will arise at some point, and when it does, remember that people can serve on a drama team in all sorts of ways that don't require acting abilities.

The *drama director* should be someone experienced in the dramatic arts who can serve in the paradoxical roles of quality-control engineer and creative visionary. Because this person is the communication link between the senior pastor and the drama ministry team, it is advisable to have one person serve in this capacity rather than several volunteers, in order to keep the vision and communication cohesive.

Responsibilities of the drama director (besides the grunt work of hauling props offstage when there's no one else to do it) include:
- effectively communicating with the senior pastor
- holding auditions for individuals interested in acting
- finding or commissioning scripts
- casting (at least until a casting volunteer is found)
- serving as the primary liaison between drama team members
- distributing approved scripts for memorization
- arranging for and conducting rehearsals
- blocking—i.e., determining movements on stage
- eliciting better performances from actors
- selecting props or communicating with prop volunteers
- stage management—i.e., making certain that the actors and props are where they need to be during the worship service
- building the team through social opportunities, prayer, and encouragement

The *actors* you seek must be servants first, which means they are in the ministry because they wish to serve God with their gifts rather than be spotlighted on stage. This is an important distinction that is surprisingly easy to detect. Are your actors eager to do all that goes along with an effective drama ministry, even when it has *nothing* to do with those few minutes on stage? The list of responsibilities includes prayer, hauling set pieces and props, making phone calls, mentoring others, and wielding a paintbrush. Servants don't criticize or disparage others in the ministry, hold grudges, or create cliques. There will be misunderstandings and difficulties, hurt feelings and misspoken words, but these should be rare events, not defining characteristics of the group. Instead, unity, friendship, forgiveness, and common purpose should pull the group together.

Support positions are also servant roles filled by talented individuals. There are numerous ways to be involved in a drama ministry. Large productions (Christmas events or dinner theatre) require a visionary production designer (someone who creates the look of the play). Also essential are prop gatherers, backdrop painters, costume designers, people who sew, media (sound) volunteers, lighting artists, and stage managers.

These individuals have less visibility than the people appearing on stage, so make efforts to thank them graciously and communicate their importance to other ministry members.

Make a Mission

With the team in place, consider your plans and purpose. Invite your team members to go through this exercise with you. State your mission, vision, and objectives. Write them down. Create a plan for at least one year. (The drama director and the senior pastor are the ones who should finalize the document.) A sample document might look like this:

MISSION:
To worship and glorify God through theatre arts.

VISION:
We aim to present thoughtful and engaging dramatic elements of the highest quality that enable participants to consider and apply spiritual insights in a new and exciting way.

OBJECTIVES:
- To draw in more worship participants
- To support the senior pastor by providing dramas that augment the week's theme or message
- To create dramatic elements that are an integral part of worship
- To create a small community for people gifted in theatre arts

Your one-year plan might include a variety of hopes and dreams:
- To prepare and present a variety of slice of life dramas, humorous vignettes, and memorized Scripture
- To provide ways for participants to improve their skills through community classes
- To incorporate other art forms wherever and whenever possible
- To grow the ministry by 10 percent in the coming year, drawing in more people who have God-given gifts in dramatic arts

Give a copy of the draft document to your pastor for input, and once it has been finalized by the senior pastor and the drama director, provide a copy to anyone who joins your team, whether an actor, painter, or costume designer. Make certain that every participant understands what is at the ministry's core. Update as necessary.

Gather High-Quality Scripts

Your scripts can be engaging, funny, serious, or experimental. Scripts perform many functions, including setting up or ending sermons, asking questions, or helping viewers recognize themselves and situations they have personally encountered. Worship dramas are most often short, between three and ten minutes, with five minutes being a comfortable average length. Steer clear of didactic or moralizing dramas. Your audience will recognize them as artificial.

Adapt scripts to meet your specific needs. Consider who in your drama ministry is available to play roles. If a particular role is written for a female, try rewriting it for a male, and vice versa. Change the names of characters or places when necessary. Make scripts work for your unique setting.

Think Creatively

Try not to "give away the ending" before the worship experience unfolds or your pastor has had a chance to speak. Consider placing scripts that provide a resolution at the end of the service or breaking them into two segments, delivering the first part before the sermon and the second part after the sermon. For a different effect, intertwine music with drama. Spend time brainstorming with media and musical staff about ways to include music, video, imagery, or sound effects.

Pursue Simplicity

Grandiose plans are a quick way to squash the productivity and enthusiasm of a talented, start-up team. Build stamina gradually, and demonstrate your reliability to pastoral staff and worship-service participants by perfecting small projects. Don't risk instant burnout by planning elaborate sets and backdrops or by bringing large casts on stage. Forget the epics. Simple is good. Begin with reader's theatre, especially Scripture. Move on to memorized Scripture, using people who have the voice and the gift. Look for opportunities to practice and build experience by presenting dramas at times other than Sunday morning: special events, family camp, Bible studies, etc. Grow and expand as your group's talent expands. As your team and experience grow, so can your productions. While worship-service dramas should remain short, you may wish to develop longer, even full-length, plays for outreach events or holiday programs.

Consider Costumes

Slice of life dramas make use of carefully selected outfits that the actors bring from home. Producing a Biblical or large-scale production requires the expertise of people gifted in design and historical reference. A blessed drama ministry includes a talented costume designer and a legion of people willing to sew. The bathrobe is dead! High-quality costumes are a worthwhile and long-lasting investment. With a committed team of volunteer tailors, your cost will be minimal.

Expect Commitment

Anticipate longevity and set up your ministry to achieve it. This expectation comes directly from your pastor. Hearing that your pastor expects this to be a long-lived ministry gives the drama director and other team participants both a positive sense of support and the burden of accountability. Commit to continuing the ministry even when you confront such difficulties as attrition, casting difficulties, surprising and discouraging amounts of set and prop hauling, and criticism. It is highly likely that you will receive criticism. Learn from constructive comments, and be prepared to overlook anonymous, inappropriate, or sour responses from lone individuals. Your pastor may, of course, wish to respond to comments and choose which are valuable to your team and which are best left unsaid. Change can be difficult for some worship participants. With your pastor's help, you'll be able to discern valid criticism from isolated gripes.

Self-Assess

After the first few months, rate your efforts. Include your pastor in this exercise. Have the dramas hit the set standards? Is your pastor feeling encouraged? Discuss frankly what could be changed or improved to keep the ministry dynamic and growing. Look again at your documentation. Is it still accurate?

Call It What It Is

Your presentations can be vignettes, comedies, slices of life, or dramas. It is best to avoid the word "skits" because the term lowers expectations of quality. Skits are done on the fly with little preparation. Calling your presentations vignettes or dramas expresses the amount of time and effort that you will be putting into your work.

Moving Ahead

Basic Requirements

When you fill the basic requirements, you're ready to launch a ministry. At a minimum you should have:
- regular prayer support from the participants as well as other volunteers
- individuals and leaders who are willing to commit to long-term and frequent participation, not to one or two times a year
- high-quality scripts
- a realistic budget for a minimum of props, costumes, and scripts

A Few Drama Types

To avoid complete volunteer burnout, don't try to present a drama each week. Plan out the year, or quarter, in advance. Which weeks would most benefit from the addition of a dramatic element? Submit a written plan to your pastor. Vary the type of drama in order to use the gifts of your team and to keep the audience interested.

READERS' THEATRE: This narration-based drama is ideal for a beginning team. There are no sets or full costumes. Actors stand or sit on chairs or stools, and they openly use scripts. You may wish to create folders or booklets to lessen the distraction of turning pages. Actors should be well-rehearsed and familiar with the script. Reading Scripture in the style of reader's theatre is an excellent way to begin your ministry.

MEMORIZED SCRIPTURE: Presenting Scripture is not a performance. It is a way of making verses come alive through skilled individuals. Consider having your speakers stand or sit someplace other than the pulpit or podium. Include natural gestures and movement when appropriate. Scripture can also be a backdrop for other action on the stage, including dance or mime. Adding music or imagery on a screen can create other layers of meaning, but don't feel that you must add anything at all. Scripture alone is powerful.

SLICE OF LIFE: Emphasizing realism and emotion in a short time frame, slice of life pieces capture a dramatic or arresting situation or conflict. Open-ended scripts are more personal and leave the viewer asking, "What would I do?"

COMEDY: To present a comedy well, you need a top-notch script and actors with an outstanding sense of timing. The tiniest gestures, facial expressions, and inflections make all the difference. Comedy is a wonderful way to diffuse difficult topics.

BIBLICAL DRAMA: Of all styles of drama, these are the most difficult to do well. Authentic costuming is an obstacle solved only with real research, time, and money. Participants must elevate their performances above the expectations of an audience that has seen one too many Christmas pageants. Don't present a reenactment of a Bible story unless you have a script that does something unexpected and thoughtful. Even the youngest children know biblical stories, so instead of simply rehashing them, rework them to give your audience a new perspective that enriches their thinking and opens doors. If you're going to take on biblical drama, consider it historical drama and pay very close attention to authentic detail.

EXPERIMENTAL: Combine music, video, dance, lighting, painting, sound effects, and other elements to heighten the impact of a drama.

POETRY: Poetry is powerful. Instead of "inspirational" rhyming poetry, trivial doggerel, or heart-warming greeting card sentiments, turn to the classics, interpret biblical poetry, or discover the depth of thought in modern poetry anthologies.

Rehearsals

The kind of rehearsal you run depends greatly on your team, but consider a healthy emphasis on efficiency. Most rehearsals, if the actors have memorized their scripts, should take an hour or less. It may take time for a fledgling ministry to get to this point, but relatively short rehearsals should be a goal. A sixty-minute rehearsal is reasonable even for very busy volunteers.

BEGIN THE REHEARSAL BY PRAYING TOGETHER. Then run through the drama at least once without stopping so the actors get a feel for the complete vignette. The director can then begin layering in blocking (as needed), stopping and starting, and rerunning problem segments.

A good actor will bring his or her own natural intuition, movements, and comedy where appropriate. A good director will bring out the best in actors by recognizing exactly what is needed at a particular point in the action onstage. There is room for dialogue between actors and the director; however, if there are disagreements, the director—as the quality control manager—should have the final say on what works and what could be improved.

A Tentative Timeline

Every church is different, and every drama team has unique needs. Allow enough time to bring out the best in your team, whatever their requirements. Use the timeline below as an example, and adjust it to suit your group.

Two months ahead:
- Get your pastor's list of upcoming sermons—a yearly, quarterly, or monthly list. Request the general topics, sermon synopses, Scripture references, and themes.
- Locate or commission scripts that will tie in closely with the sermon topics.
- Provide scripts to your pastor for approval.
- Cast dramas, contingent on the pastor's approval of scripts.

Six weeks ahead:
- Receive your pastor's approval (or changes) for submitted scripts.

Four weeks ahead:
- Confirm your cast.
- Distribute scripts to actors for memorization.
- Provide scripts to appropriate personnel (media, etc.).
- Gather props.

Two weeks ahead:
- Confirm that actors have the script memorized.
- Conduct the first rehearsal in the presentation space (if possible) with actual props and costumes. (Note: This rehearsal is optional. Once your team is experienced, you may decide that you need just one rehearsal, a week or less ahead of the worship service.)

One week ahead:
- Rehearse.

Sunday presentation:
- Meet the actors at least an hour before the worship service. (This is the director's responsibility.)
- Set the stage with props.
- Place microphones, as appropriate.
- Run the drama.
- Pray together.

The Only Rules

FOCUS ON GOD. Stay centered by making sure all of your efforts are about worship. Keep humility at the core of your ministry. Reinforcing this goal will affect all of your work and change how your actors feel walking out on the platform.

MEMORIZATION IS MANDATORY. Lines should be memorized by the first rehearsal. This allows the director to focus on blocking, line delivery, and building the comfort level of all the actors, rather than on running lines over and over. Actors rely on each other to provide verbal and physical cues, so it is vital that each person arrive at the rehearsal prepared and knowing the precise, not general, language of the script.

THE SCRIPT HAS TO WORK. A bad script can bring down even the best actors, but how do you know when it's bad? Test the quality of your script. Does it match the caliber of the rest of the service, including music and the sermon? Language that is stilted, moralistic, simplistic, or overly dramatic will make your audience feel uncomfortable and embarrassed. Make sure that the writing is professional—that is, "natural" rather than "written." Avoid Christian jargon or inside jokes that may make visitors to your service feel confused or excluded.

The best dramas raise questions instead of answering them, encouraging worshipers to ask themselves, "What would I do in a situation like this?" This approach to writing keeps the script from becoming heavy-handed, trite, didactic, or preachy. A loving, nonjudgmental approach ensures that viewers are drawn in rather than turned away. The writing should make people think more deeply about their faith, not feel guilty. God can use guilt to motivate people, but making the audience feel guilty is not the ultimate goal of your drama.

MINIMALISM MAY BE BETTER THAN ATTEMPTED REALISM. When planning props, consider what you can omit. A chair and lamp convey a living room. A bench becomes the park. Viewers fill in the details, and the simple scene is more believable than anything other than full scale realism, which is difficult to produce on a tight budget and a small stage. Less is sometimes more.

DIVERSE CHARACTERS ON STAGE APPEAL TO A DIVERSE AUDIENCE. By casting individuals who represent diverse genders, races, and ages (from children to seniors), you reflect a world that people can recognize and identify with. You can portray both Christians and nonbelievers, but they needn't always be the good guys and the antagonists, respectively. The diversity of your acting pool dictates the diversity of your casts, so hold regular auditions to increase the number in the pool.

TALENT MATTERS. The director of every drama group will eventually face the painful question, "What if a volunteer desperately wants to act but lacks the skill?" A good heart isn't enough. Every individual has been given gifts, and those gifts should take each person into areas of ministry that fit his or her skills. Fear of hurting peoples' feelings should not cause you to lower your standards for the ministry. Find ways of including people in other parts of the drama ministry, or use people on stage in small or non-speaking roles.

Prepare to deal with prima donnas, control freaks, and naysayers. Argumentative actors or people interested in the limelight will not make good additions to your ministry, no matter how talented they are.

GIFTS CAN BE DEVELOPED OVER TIME. Provide opportunities for team members to grow their gifts. Small parts, roles in dramas that aren't part of worship services, and skill-building classes all contribute to developing confidence and experience.

PEOPLE WILL COME AND GO. There's a natural attrition that occurs in any ministry effort. While it may be disheartening to be turned down, you'll soon see a pattern of God bringing new people forward.

REWARDS ARE IMPORTANT. Retain and reward your core team—the ones who are somehow always available and always willing to help out. These are the sturdy individuals you lean on, volunteers who need a minimum of handholding. You'll know them when you see them: If there's a call for volunteers, they show up. They don't differentiate between the service of acting and the service of painting backdrops or breaking down sets. These are your core members. While you continue to add gifted members to the roster, your core members should be nurtured and rewarded. Team-building efforts (dinners together, outings, etc.) help people feel they're part of a group that cares about them.

NEVER PRESENT ANYTHING BUT YOUR ABSOLUTE BEST. This offering is for the Lord.

SCRIPTS

MOST LIKELY TO HAVE REGRETS

SYNOPSIS:
Joe and Brian meet again at a high school reunion. Although always considered the guy "most likely to make millions," Joe has deep regrets.

THEMES:
Second chances
Regrets
God's plans for our lives
Starting over

CHARACTERS:
Brian, former school buddy of Joe
Joe, former school buddy of Brian

PROPS:
Name tags

(*Optional*)
Banner
Table
Tablecloth
Punchbowl and glasses
Bowls of snacks
Napkins
Other party goods

COSTUMES:
Joe—an expensive suit
Brian—a more casual suit coat and trousers

SETTING:
A school gym. A banner reads, "Welcome class of '77!" (Adjust the year to fit your cast.) A tablecloth covers a table on which a punch bowl filled with brightly colored punch, punch glasses, and other party fare are arranged.

SOUND EFFECTS: *(optional) Introduction to a song specifically from the era*

(JOE enters self-consciously. He goes to the punch bowl and pours himself a cup. He drinks, looking around. BRIAN enters.)

BRIAN: Joe? Joey Hammond?

JOE: Brian Thorpe!

(They shake hands enthusiastically.)

BRIAN: Man, I didn't think I'd see *you* here. Where have you been all these years? How have you been?

JOE: I've been—fine. You?

BRIAN: Great, great. Wait till I tell the guys you're here. We thought you'd fallen off the face of the earth. Every five-year reunion we'd get together and try to imagine what exotic place Joey Hammond was living in at the time.

JOE: This is the first time I've made a point of being in the States during the reunion.

BRIAN: So, you're in international business, right? Where are you living now?

JOE: China, at the moment.

BRIAN: *(shaking his head admiringly)* Man. You sure lived up to everyone's expectations. Joe Hammond. "Most Likely to Make Millions."

JOE: *(uncomfortable)* Right. So tell me about your life. You still living in town?

BRIAN: Oh, yeah. Teaching at the university science department. As expected.

JOE: Thorpe the brain! You followed your dream, didn't you? Stayed true to it.

BRIAN: Yeah. In spite of all the aggravation and the politics, I still love it. So where's Sherry? I'd love to catch up with her too.

JOE: *(uncomfortable)* I couldn't say. We split up years ago.

BRIAN: Oh. I'm really sorry to hear that.

JOE: It wasn't her fault; it was me, just to be clear. I made some serious mistakes. Frankly, my mistakes with Sherry were just the beginning of my wrong moves. Maybe the yearbook should have said "Joe Hammond. Most Likely to Have Regrets." If I could go back in time, start over—

BRIAN: Listen, everyone makes mistakes. I could have gone into something a little more—I don't know, lucrative.

JOE: I'm not talking about my job, Brian. I mean the life. I was so self-confident. Remember all the big talk? I got so caught up in my own abilities that I didn't give God any room for leading me. You know what the hardest part is? I'll never know what God had in mind for me.

BRIAN: But life's not over yet. Make a change.

JOE: It's too late for that.

BRIAN: Don't you believe in second chances? That's what forgiveness is all about. Ask for the forgiveness you need, and then be bold. Move ahead. See what God has in store for you.

JOE: Second best?

BRIAN: No. God's best for you now. Come on. Let me reintroduce you to the guys. They won't believe you're really here.

JOE: Thorpe the brain. What did I do without you all these years?

BRIAN: I'll never know.

(They exit.)

THE STRENGTH OF HER CONVICTIONS

SYNOPSIS:
As Becky prepares to leave on a charitable mission to a dangerous part of the world, her worried mother struggles with the idea of letting her go.

THEMES:
God's faithfulness
Victory
Missions
Courage

CHARACTERS:
Becky, a young attorney
Ava, her mother

COSTUMES:
Becky—jeans or sweats
Ava—casual pants and top

PROPS:
Suitcase
Gray sweatshirt
Miscellaneous clothing
Couch
Chair

SETTING:
A bedroom. There is an open suitcase on a chair.

(BECKY is packing, folding clothing and placing it in the suitcase. She's hurrying, rather disorganized. Her mother enters, peering into the room.)

AVA: Yoo-hoo. I'm here.

BECKY: You're early. We don't have to leave for the airport for another hour.

AVA: I wanted to spend some time with you before you go. I won't get in the way.

BECKY: All right, come in. But you're just going to see how disorganized I am.

AVA: I'm your mother. I know you're a slob.

(She follows BECKY, who returns to packing. AVA stands watching her. After a pause—)

AVA: You're really doing this.

BECKY: Yes.

AVA: I still don't understand. It's a committee of attorneys or something?

BECKY: *(She's explained this before, so a little impatience shows.)* No, Mom. It's a nonprofit organization made up of attorneys. We provide free legal services to political prisoners and victims of torture.

AVA: Well, is there no one else to do this kind of work? Lawyers with more experience? Why do they have to send a young person like you?

BECKY: There are all kinds of people involved. Experienced attorneys. Young attorneys. And no, it doesn't *have* to be me. But I *want* to go.

AVA: Well, can someone guarantee your safety? I would like some assurances—

BECKY: I told you. There are no guarantees in this work. *(She realizes she sounds harsh. She stops for a moment to address her mother eye-to-eye* *and squeeze her arm.)* But I won't be alone. *(distracted)* Where's my gray sweatshirt?

AVA: Right here. *(She picks up the sweatshirt and folds it carefully, then places the sweatshirt in the suitcase. In a smaller voice—)* It's such a long way. And I was reading in the paper again this morning that there's so much—violence there. Three kidnappings last month alone. You've been reading the paper haven't you? You know what's happening there?

BECKY: *(laughing gently)* Yes, I know.

AVA: Right now it's the native residents disappearing. Next it could be visiting foreigners. Even foreigners on "charitable" missions.

BECKY: It's the right thing to do.

AVA: *(starting to realize she can't talk Becky out of her decision)* You always have to solve the world's problems.

BECKY: I can't solve this, Mom. But God is more powerful than the evil there. My job isn't to solve the world's problems, just to listen to God.

(AVA is silent; she can't argue.)

I keep picturing what it will be like when it's over. People celebrating in the streets, no longer afraid to go to bed at night. Can you imagine that?

AVA: *(desperately)* I'm trying.

BECKY: I can picture it clear as day.

(They freeze. Exit.)

JUST A COUPLE OF COINS

SYNOPSIS:
A man is stranded on a hot day after his car breaks down. He is offered help by a homeless woman, the same woman he drives by every day without offering any money. She sacrificially gives him two quarters to make a phone call for a tow truck.

THEMES:
Sharing
Homelessness
Caring for the needy
Accepting help
Doing good for our enemies

CHARACTERS:
Homeless woman
Wealthy man

COSTUMES:
Man—rumpled suit
Woman—casual clothing, but not obviously the costume of a homeless person

PROPS:
Coins (2 quarters)

SETTING:
Deserted street

(*MAN enters. His hair and clothing are noticeably disheveled. He is carrying his coat over his shoulder, muttering to himself. He is hot and irritable. WOMAN enters, sees him and watches him with interest. Amused, she calls out . . .*)

WOMAN: Hey! You!

MAN: (*heavily, with forced politeness*) Pardon me, ma'am, but I am not in the mood for any hassles right now.

WOMAN: Me, hassle you? Not likely. You look cranky. I avoid cranky people.

MAN: Good.

WOMAN: Having a terrible day, huh?

MAN: What was your first clue?

WOMAN: Yeah, I'm a pretty shrewd judge of character.

MAN: And does your shrewd judgment also tell you that my car just ran out of gas?

WOMAN: Ooh, major bummer.

MAN: It's the Fourth of July, the gas stations are all closed, (*shaking cell phone*) and my cell phone is dead. Of all the fantastic timing!

WOMAN: I've had days like that.

MAN: Oh, please, I beg you, no examples.

WOMAN: I was going to help.

MAN: Just tell me where I can find the nearest pay phone.

WOMAN: (*pointing*) Three or four miles down (local street or road).

MAN: Three or four miles?

WOMAN: More or less.

MAN: Just great!

(*He starts to exit, frustrated.*)

WOMAN: (*calling*) I hope you get your wheels back.

MAN: (*sarcastically*) Thanks a million.

(*WOMAN continues in opposite direction. Suddenly MAN groans loudly and stops.*)

WOMAN: What?

MAN: I don't have any change. To make the phone call. (*He throws down his coat and sinks down in despair and frustration.*)

WOMAN: Man, you're in tough shape. (*She thinks about it a second.*) Hey, I know you.

MAN: No, you don't.

WOMAN: Sure, I do. I know people by their cars. What do you drive? Come on, what do you drive?

White Lexus! You're the white Lexus!

(*MAN stares at her.*)

MAN: How do you know that?

WOMAN: Oh, you know me, too. My beat is at the top of the freeway exit on North Fifth Street, downtown. You drive by me every day. Left-hand lane. I'm the one with the sign?

(*He stands up. Obviously he does not comprehend.*)

WOMAN: (*gesturing to imaginary sign that she's holding in front of herself*) "Homeless. Broke. Please help. God bless."

(*Uncomfortable beat.*)

MAN: That's you?

WOMAN: Well, sure!

MAN: (*holding up his hand as if to ward her off*) Don't bother asking. I don't have any money. I'm penniless! (*MAN says this angrily, defensively.*)

WOMAN: Yeah, I know. (*Pauses while she thinks.*) Here. (*WOMAN digs into her pocket and extends her hand to him.*)

(*MAN draws back instinctively.*)

MAN: What?

WOMAN: Change.

(*MAN looks at the money uncomprehendingly.*)

For the phone call?

MAN: I thought you didn't have any money.

WOMAN: I don't—until some guy rolls down his window and gives me some. Just so happens Mr. Grey Audi came by today. He always shares a couple of bucks. Take it. (*WOMAN places two quarters in his palm.*)

MAN: Don't you need it?

WOMAN: Yeah, I need it. But you take it.

(*MAN rises, takes money. WOMAN starts to exit.*)

MAN: I don't know what to say.

WOMAN: *(she laughs)* Whatever.

MAN: I never thought I'd be so happy to see a couple of quarters. Well, this is great. Really great. Thanks.

WOMAN: That's okay, Mr. White Lexus. I'll be seeing you.

(WOMAN exits.)

MAN: Right. *(He looks at coins in his palm as she exits.)* Right. *(He lifts his head and looks after her, still holding his palm open with the coins.)*

(MAN exits.)

IN SEARCH OF . . .

SYNOPSIS:
On a golf outing, Diane and Mike (brother and sister) again fall into a discussion of how Diane will not forgive a past wrong of their sister.

THEMES:
Forgiveness
Family difficulties
Past pain
Holding grudges

CHARACTERS:
Diane, sister
Mike, brother

COSTUMES:
Diane and Mike—casual clothing

PROPS:
Golf bags (2)
Golf clubs
Table
Chairs (2)
Thermos or pitcher
Cups
PDA or BlackBerry™

SETTING:
The clubhouse off the greenway

(DIANE enters, lugging golf clubs. She pauses to wipe sweat from her brow. Then she shoulders the golf clubs again and staggers toward the stage. She unceremoniously deposits the bag in a heap. MIKE enters and walks down the aisle, carrying a golf bag with ease.)

MIKE: Wait up, Diane. Hey, sis!

DIANE: *(teasingly)* I know why you brought me out here today. You were trying to take away my last scrap of self worth. That was your little scheme, wasn't it?

MIKE: Hey, for a first time out, you weren't so bad. I've seen worse. *(He finally lets out all his pent-up laughter.)* Okay, you *were* the worst! I have never seen anything like it! Was that for real? Talk about entertainment value! Wow. Oh, don't sulk. I'm sorry. Sit down with me and have a nice glass of lemonade. Brother to sister.

DIANE: Lemonade is not going to make up for personal humiliation. All right. Fill it to the top. You owe me *big time*.

(They take seats at a metal or wooden table. MIKE pours lemonade from a thermos into cups.)

MIKE: Seriously, it was fun. It's been a long time since we've hung out. We could get together next week. Saturday afternoon. Hey, we can go rollerblading around Lake Calhoun. *(wickedly)* Wait, wait, I've got it. Bungee jumping!

DIANE: Nope. After today, I'm going back to my life of ease.

MIKE: All right. Something less strenuous. *(checking PDA or BlackBerry)* Let's have lunch. Saturday, the twenty-seventh. We could get some Vietnamese food at that place near your condo.

DIANE: Sure. And we could watch those old family movies I had transferred to video.

MIKE: Oh, yeah. That's great! Okay, now don't bite my head off. How about if I invite Renee?

DIANE: What? Oh, no, you're not going to start that again.

MIKE: But Diane, she's our little sister. Don't you think after all this time we should let up a little?

DIANE: I'm tuning you out, Mike. (*She puts her fingers in her ears. MIKE stares at her. She takes her fingers out of her ears. She picks up her glass. After a pause—*) I can feel your beady little eyes boring into my brain.

MIKE: We have to talk.

DIANE: Oh—the "Let the past be the past, forgive and forget" lecture again.

MIKE: How'd you know what I was going to say?

DIANE: I've known you for a million years. Listen, save your breath. You have to face it. Renee and I are not best friends like we were when we were kids—

MIKE: Best friends? You're not even talking anymore—

DIANE: (*angrily*) And that makes you uncomfortable.

MIKE: This is about you and Renee. You don't even seem to care about her anymore.

DIANE: I *don't* care about her. I can't. It's too dangerous. (*confused*) No, of course I care about her. But I'll never trust her again.

MIKE: I don't blame you.

DIANE: Yes, you do. You think I'm the one standing in the way of a joyful family reunion. Everything could be made alright if I would just open my heart to her. Fling open the doors! Invite her back into my life so she can cause more damage! That's what she's good at!

MIKE: Di-anne. I know it's not that easy. And I don't think your forgiveness is some sort of magic potion. But staying mad at her isn't helping. It's especially not helping you. *(admitting)* I'm mad at her too, you know.

DIANE: You? What'd she do to you?

MIKE: She hurt my sister.

DIANE: And she's not even sorry!

MIKE: I know.

DIANE: I'm giving up on her, Mike. I don't have it in me to forget the past. Maybe if she came begging. If I heard her admit that she's sorry. If she acknowledged for one minute all the pain she's brought into this family—

MIKE: *(softly)* Don't wait for her. You can't control her. Just do what you can do. Forgive her.

DIANE: *(jumping up, furious)* Why do you want me to make all the moves when you know it's her fault?

MIKE: It's the only way things will ever change. For you.

DIANE: *(cornered)* I can't do it! I'm not holy like you. You forgive her!

MIKE: I'm going to try. With God's help I'm going to try.

DIANE: How can you forget what she did?

MIKE: I can't. And I don't expect you to. But forgiving—maybe that's possible. Maybe.

(Tension. They're both still for a moment.)

It doesn't matter what she does any more. Only what we do.

(They freeze. Exit.)

FROM THE HEART

SYNOPSIS:
Josh and Adam tell their stories. Josh's is a faith story about how God transformed him. Adam's is the story of moving into a new town and feeling lonely. Josh tries to befriend him. Although Adam never lets down his guard, he is intrigued by this young man's unconditional friendship.

THEMES:
Love
Unconditional friendship
Transformation
Getting past the "attitude" of others
Heart over mind
Christian love
Coping with difficult times
Christ-like behavior

CHARACTERS:
Josh, a high school boy
Adam, the same age

COSTUMES:
Josh and Adam—typical high school student clothing

PROPS:
Books
Backpacks

SETTING:
High school hallway or classroom

(JOSH and ADAM and take their positions. They stand facing the audience, parallel but not close. They may carry books or backpacks.)

JOSH: I became a Christian in junior high. Up until then, I didn't know much about God. I went to church and considered myself a good person, but I was no different from my friends. When I asked Christ into my life, my blurry faith became sharp and clear. I won't say I never had another problem, but a lot of things fell into place for me. Faith stopped being an abstract idea and became something very real in my life. Something that had to be practiced. Lived.

ADAM: Last year was "the big move." The worst thing that ever happened to me. From the first day in the school, I knew it. The kids here are complete losers. Totally backward. If they had shown up at my old school, we would have laughed them off campus.

JOSH: I knew what was expected of someone who said he loved Jesus. For the first time, I felt different from my friends, who seemed to go any way the crowd went. If everyone else drank till they were sick, they'd do it too. If someone bragged about cheating on an exam, they all thought it was okay. For me, becoming a Christian showed me that it really mattered what I said and what I did.

ADAM: You want to hear the saddest part? They all treated me like I was the lower life form. How stupid is that? They were the freaks and I was the one treated like an outsider. From day one it seemed like everyone hated me.

JOSH: My faith came in handy this year after I met Adam. New kid.

ADAM: Well, there was one guy who tried to be friendly. Named Josh. He would talk to me.

JOSH: No one had much to do with Adam. I could hardly blame them. He had this attitude. You just couldn't get through it. He was always talking about his old school and his old friends. But I felt sorry for him. It seemed like everyone knew he was lonely and vulnerable, and they made him the scapegoat. Pretending to be super-nice but only to humiliate him. Like he was too dumb to notice. Or insulting him right to his face. So I went out of my way to be his friend.

ADAM: This guy never gave up. Always trying to prove how perfect he was. I think he was some sort of religious freak.

JOSH: I can't say I really wanted to be his friend. But in another way, I did. It's hard to explain. My mind said no, but my heart pushed me ahead. One thing is sure: He didn't want me for a friend. He wanted to make me suffer as much as he was suffering.

ADAM: What was this guy after? I didn't want to talk with him, or anybody. I just wanted to be left alone.

JOSH: I was patient because I knew what he was going through. The kids at school were always on him. No one would sit with him at lunch. If he sat down at a table, they'd get up and leave.

ADAM: He started trying to eat lunch with me. But I always cut him off. I didn't need his pity.

JOSH: It was like he was determined not to let me get too close. I knew I was doing the right thing. But why was it so hard? I prayed about it. "Why aren't you breaking down any barriers, God?"

ADAM: I hate them all. I just want to get out of here—and go back home.

JOSH: I wish I could just help him relax. Take a breath and realize it's not so bad here. He could make friends. I could help him. But maybe it doesn't matter whether I can help him or not. Maybe like the Bible says, what I'm supposed to do is love my brother deeply from the heart.

ADAM: I wonder about that Josh sometimes. How'd he get to be the way he is?

JOSH: How did *I* become the kind of person who can show Christ's love? Even to someone like Adam?

(They freeze. Exit.)

BABY STEPS

SYNOPSIS:
After a church service, Pat admits to Cecile that a mutual friend named Bev makes her nervous. It appears to Pat that Bev has her spiritual life all put together. Cecile suggests that Pat take baby steps toward her goal of becoming more mature in her faith.

THEMES:
Spiritual growth
Feelings of spiritual inadequacy
Taking in spiritual milk
Small steps toward holiness

CHARACTERS:
Cecile
Pat

COSTUMES:
Cecile and Pat—typical church attire

PROPS:
Bibles

(*Optional*)
Service programs
Coats

Setting:
Church, just following the worship service

SOUND EFFECTS: (optional) Musical postlude

(PAT and CECILE enter together, talking and laughing.)

CECILE: Great service, huh?

PAT: Yeah. I always leave church feeling so up. It really helps me start my week on the right track.

CECILE: Thanks for letting me claim that empty seat next to you, Pat. It's getting hard to find a place to sit in this service.

PAT: No problem. Wasn't the faith story amazing today?

CECILE: I got choked up!

PAT: You always sniffle during that part of the service!

CECILE: I can't help it. It's really encouraging to hear how regular people experience God's supernatural power.

PAT: It sure is.

CECILE: Look, there's Bev. *(waving)* Hey, Bev!

PAT: Um, Cecile, would you mind not calling Bev over here?

CECILE: Why not?

PAT: I like her, but—to be honest, she makes me really uncomfortable.

CECILE: You're kidding.

PAT: No—she's so superior.

CECILE: I've never gotten that impression.

PAT: I don't mean she acts superior. She *is* superior. She has her spiritual life together. She never struggles in the practice of her faith—like me. Compared to her, I'm just a big Christian slug. I never get very far, and I leave a slimy trail wherever I go.

CECILE: *(laughs)* Pat, what are you talking about?

PAT: *(also taking a seat)* I know I'm being ridiculous! But it's not just Bev. It's people like her. They're everywhere! People who know the Bible. Who can pray out loud in a group without sounding stupid. I get so self-conscious if I'm asked to pray, all I can think of is "thank you for this food." I just feel inadequate. I'm tired of being a novice around pros. *(wistfully)* I wish I could be like her. So—perfect.

(CECILE laughs.)

PAT: You're laughing again.

CECILE: I've known Bev for a long time. She's far from perfect.

PAT: Oh, come on! The church staff trusts her to teach Sunday school. She can recite the books of the Bible. She probably has a Bible quote for any occasion—the birth of a baby, a big promotion, even the death of the family hamster. She's so comforting, she makes me sick. Admit it. You know it's true.

CECILE: It's not magic, you know. Bev had to grow to get where she is now. You could do it too. Strength of faith isn't just for "some people." Anyone can grow stronger in her walk if she's willing to take the steps.

PAT: What steps?

CECILE: Out with the bad, in with the good. *(touching her Bible)* The Bible says we should avoid things like "malice . . . deceit . . . hypocrisy . . . envy . . . slander—"

PAT: See? You're quoting Scripture, too.

CECILE: —and start craving spiritual milk.

PAT: *(lightly sarcastic) That* sounds easy.

CECILE: We can start by replacing the junk in our lives with good things that help us grow in our spiritual walk.

PAT: Like what?

CECILE: Have you ever heard of the discipleship program? Where you meet with a mentor one-on-one? Or maybe you could join a Bible study? Or just start reading your Bible every day? There are a lot of steps you could start to take.

PAT: I'm not ready for this.

CECILE: It's just little steps. You'll hardly notice.

(They exit.)

A NEAR MISS

SYNOPSIS:
After a hit-and-run accident, Rose (sister of David) has to face the reality of her brother's near death and her own lack of preparation for disaster.

THEMES:
Living as if tomorrow is your last day
Death
Near-death experiences
Preparation for death
No regrets

CHARACTERS:
David, the brother
Rose, the sister

COSTUMES:
David and Rose—casual clothing

PROPS:
Cell phone
Bench

SETTING:
Curb on a busy street

(ROSE and DAVID enter. ROSE is trying to help DAVID walk, although he's resisting. She carries a cell phone.)

DAVID: *(winded)* Rose. Rose! I'm alright.

(She finds the bench and forces him to sit down.)

ROSE: *(dials 911)* I need to report an accident. My brother was just hit by a car—a hit and run. Just now. Girard and 35th. David Lester. Yes, he's conscious. And talking, yes. *(checking him over)* No blood. How long is the ambulance going to take?

DAVID: It didn't hit me hard. Not hard enough to break any bones.

ROSE: He and I were crossing the street with the light and this guy came out of nowhere and turned left on top of us. It was a red Mustang. That's all I remember. No, I didn't get a license number. I was too scared to think. Yes, we'll be right here. Please hurry!

(She ends the call.)

(to DAVID) Are you sure you're alright?

DAVID: Yes. Just let me get my breath.

ROSE: This is a nightmare! Where's that ambulance?

DAVID: It'll be here soon. Take deep breaths.

(ROSE starts to follow his instruction and then realizes what she's doing.)

ROSE: I'm not the one who was almost killed. You should be doing the deep breathing.

DAVID: I feel fine. Although there was a moment there— As the car came toward me I heard my mind say, "This is it." Clear as anything.

ROSE: *(urgently)* Where were you hit?

(DAVID indicates his side.)

What if you had been killed? You came so close. *(Emotion overtakes her.)*

DAVID: Look—I'm still here. Feistier than ever. I'll be pestering you a while longer.

ROSE: *(rising)* How can you be so calm? David, you're freaking me out.

DAVID: But Rose, if it happened today, I would have been ready. *(trying to make himself clear)* Not ready to leave—but prepared.

ROSE: *(tensely)* I'm not even going to talk with you about this. *(She sits down next to him. They're silent for a moment. ROSE's curiosity gets the best of her.)*

All right, what do you mean prepared? You have your will in order, that sort of thing?

DAVID: No. I have my life in order.

ROSE: No one's ever prepared for—

DAVID: *(Sighing and rubbing his side)* I try to live a life free of regret by doing what I know is right. What God wants. Being honest even when it hurts. Serving God without griping. Being kind—even to my enemies.

ROSE: You don't have any enemies.

DAVID: *(significantly)* I know.

ROSE: I try to live right, too, but I don't have that kind of peace. I can't think of anything scarier than being killed. There'd be so many things I hadn't done yet. And so many mistakes to correct.

DAVID: I put God first. The other stuff comes naturally.

ROSE: It's easy for you, isn't it?

DAVID: Of course not. But I never doubt that I'm doing the right thing. And I am ready for just about anything.

ROSE: *(She looks at him admiringly)* I've always wanted to be like you, David. Thank God you're okay.

DAVID: We both know the end is near. We just don't know *how* near.

ROSE: How's your pulse? *(putting her fingers on his wrist)*

DAVID: Cut it out, Rose!

ROSE: I hear ambulance sirens.

DAVID: It was just a near miss. Today we start fresh.

(They freeze. Exit.)

READY AND WAITING

SYNOPSIS:
A journalist interviews a successful author about her work and life, noting her ability to deal with difficult times.

THEMES:
Problems
Suffering
Issues from childhood
Overcoming bitterness
Dealing with the difficulties of life

CHARACTERS:
Journalist, a professional young man
Author, a mature woman with great poise and grace

COSTUMES:
Journalist—khakis, nice shirt
Author—something uniquely "her" (not a costume, but the tasteful apparel of someone confident in herself)

PROPS:
Steno notebook
Pen
Chairs (2)
Coffee table
A thick, hardcover novel

(AUTHOR leads JOURNALIST into the room and indicates a chair.)

AUTHOR: Why don't we meet in here?

JRNLST: Great.

(There are two chairs with a coffee table between them. The novel is on the table. JOURNALIST sits and opens his steno pad. His posture indicates that he is in the presence of a person of note. AUTHOR sits beside him.)

JRNLST: Thank you so much for granting me some of your time today. I know how busy you are.

AUTHOR: *(very gracious)* I'm happy to help. This interview fell conveniently between book tours. But I certainly hope you've been warned. I give lousy interviews. They make me nervous.

JRNLST: Being interviewed makes you uncomfortable? After all you've accomplished? *(He picks up the novel and weighs it in his hand. Then he leans forward eagerly to hear what the author is saying.)*

AUTHOR: Most of the journalists with whom I speak sit forward in their chairs waiting for me to say something witty and quotable.

(JOURNALIST realizes he is sitting forward in his chair. He sits back and tries to appear casual.)

The pressure of being clever always makes me . . . itchy. *(As he begins to write—)* Oh, you're not going to write that down are you?

JRNLST: Sorry. *(scribbles over the notation)*

AUTHOR: *(continuing to scratch unconsciously)* Well, go ahead. I'll do my best.

JRNLST: *(consulting his notes)* Okay. Anyone who writes the intense books that you write must do so from a depth of life experience. But not a lot has been published about your personal life. You had a very painful childhood, I understand.

AUTHOR: I haven't spoken much about it.

JRNLST: There's speculation that your characters are really stand-ins for yourself—

AUTHOR: Yes, everyone assumes that authors are writing about themselves. *(pointing to the notebook)* Maybe you could explode that myth in your article.

JRNLST: But it's obvious that some of the situations you write about are ones you are personally familiar with. I can't help wondering how you can write about such painful things without bitterness—I mean, the abuse that you endured.

AUTHOR: Perhaps you've heard about my faith—

JRNLST: Yes, I understand that you're a committed Christian. But no matter your religious beliefs, don't you ever ask "Why me?"

AUTHOR: I am much more interested in "Now what?"

JRNLST: What does that mean?

AUTHOR: We're surrounded by trouble, you know. I stay braced for it— not expecting it pessimistically, but never surprised when it appears.

JRNLST: I think you're pretty amazing.

AUTHOR: Don't be ridiculous. And don't you dare put that in your article.

(JOURNALIST'S pen stops.)

JRNLST: Why not?

AUTHOR: Because I'm not special.

JRNLST: But it does seem that you have a unique strength—

AUTHOR: What's unique about me? Like everyone else, I avoid pain. I just always "have my bag packed," just in case.

JRNLST: You were treated for serious health problems last year—

AUTHOR: Cancer, yes.

JRNLST: Even then—?

AUTHOR: Did I feel persecuted or "singled out"? No. Maybe if I were the only person on the planet with trouble! But there's pain, neglect, and difficulty everywhere you look. We are born into it. *(as an aside, with humor)* At least as a writer I can always use the pain in my work!

JRNLST: *(again poising his pencil)* Aha! So the books *are* based on your life!

AUTHOR: You know, you're a better interviewer than I thought you'd be.

JRNLST: *(smiling)* Just doing my job, ma'am.

(They freeze. Exit.)

A Changed Man

SYNOPSIS:
Worried about the possibility of losing his job, Mark almost allows his anxiety and anger to keep him from spending time with his young son.

THEMES:
Worry
Anxiety
Job loss
Family life
Father's Day
Spending time with children
The peace of God
Trust

CHARACTERS:
Mark, stressed-out father
Leslie, his wife
Isaac, his son (preteen or early teen)

COSTUMES:
Mark, Leslie, and Isaac—casual clothing

PROPS:
Bucket
Cleaning supplies
Handmade card
Five-dollar bill
Frisbee
Kite
Baseball mitts (2)
Baseball
Bin or box

SETTING:
The driveway outside of Mark and Leslie's home

(MARK is loading cleaning supplies into a bucket. LESLIE enters.)

LESLIE: Mark, what are you doing?

MARK: Getting ready to wash the car.

LESLIE: On Father's Day? Why don't you take a break? Do something fun. Take Isaac with you.

MARK: I can't relax. I have to do something.

LESLIE: *(going to him sympathetically)* You have to stop worrying about your job. It's going to work out.

MARK: *(mildly sarcastic)* Thanks. I wish I could share your optimism, but I told you, things have never been so bad at the company. I almost wish they'd just get it over with. Put us out of our misery.

LESLIE: *(helplessly—half trying to convince herself)* We've been through downturns before. You've always come through them okay.

MARK: *(suddenly angry)* I told you this layoff is different. It's my neck out there.

(LESLIE draws back. MARK feels instant regret.)

I'm sorry, Leslie. I'm sorry.

LESLIE: I only want to make you feel better.

MARK: I know. I'm so sorry.

LESLIE: What can I do? I'm helpless.

MARK: *(putting his arms around her)* Me, too.

(*LESLIE pulls away and exits. MARK watches her go, then goes back to loading the bucket, feeling defeated. ISAAC enters carrying sporting equipment in a bin or box.*)

ISAAC: Here, Dad.

MARK: What's all this?

ISAAC: Your Father's Day present! (*hands his father a homemade card*)

MARK: (*reading*) "You're the best. Your gift this year is a whole day of play—with me. Yours truly. Your wonderful son, Isaac." (*MARK pulls a five-dollar bill out of the card.*)

ISAAC: That's for ice cream cones. Later.

MARK: Well, thanks. This is just great! We'll have to set a date. Real soon.

ISAAC: No, it's for today. We're gonna spend the afternoon having fun. First—(*shows frisbee*) wild frisbee. Then—(*shows kite*) kite flying. (*Pulls out two mitts and baseball.*) Thought we could throw a ball around. Come on, Dad. Just you and me!

MARK: (*understanding that he has to be careful not to hurt his son's feelings, but reluctant to give up his plans*) I was going to wash the car.

ISAAC: (*disappointed*) Oh. After that.

MARK: (*deciding*) Maybe another day, Isaac. I just don't feel much like celebrating.

ISAAC: But it's Father's Day! Tomorrow will be just another day.

(*MARK motions for ISAAC to join him on the step. They sit down.*)

MARK: I— I haven't shared anything like this with you before. Your mom and I are facing a really . . . scary situation. There's a layoff coming at work. This time, I'm pretty sure I'm going to be one of the cuts. It's almost a sure thing. If that happens— (*he stops himself*) So that's why I'm not in the mood to play. I can't really think about much else.

ISAAC: Oh.

(ISAAC looks at MARK and slaps his knee gently. Having explained himself, MARK wearily stands up and returns to his task.)

ISAAC: Dad, there's something that I've never talked about with you either.

MARK: *(taken aback; a little nervously—)* What?

ISAAC: Something I've been learning about. Sort of an experiment. Maybe it'd work for you. Since you can't control your situation at work, you might try something more—powerful.

MARK: Anxiety exercises? I'm way past that, Isaac. This is not some little problem. This affects everything. Our life today. Our plans for the future.

ISAAC: *(getting excited)* I know. I'm talking about something BIG. Something MEGA-POWERFUL.

MARK: Yeah?

ISAAC: God control. Like you hand all of your scared feelings to God—and not just like you *say* you give it to God. You really *do* it. You let God be in control. Then—*(delivering the coupe de grace)*—you don't get to think about it anymore.

MARK: I told you, Isaac. I'm way past anxiety exercises. This is a life-changing problem.

ISAAC: *(impatiently)* No, no. I told you. God control. We're talking about the God of the Universe! *(seeing his father's blank stare)* Okay, so you know God loves you, right? And if the God of the Universe loves you, then what?

MARK: I let God do God's thing?

ISAAC: I think so. I don't know how it all works either, but God is supposed to take on the worry. And you get— Well, there's this "peace of God, which transcends all understanding." It guards your heart and your mind.

You want to try this, Dad? You can help me. I'm just getting into it myself. It sounds crazy to me too, but if it's written in the Bible, there must be something to it.

MARK: I'd forgotten about those verses. (*touched by his son's enthusiasm, amused, and also convicted*) Yes. Let me put away this stuff. (*He picks up the cleaning materials.*) Come on.

ISAAC: This is so cool. What are we doing?

MARK: Frisbee.

ISAAC: (*thrilled—bursting out*) Really?

MARK: Let's call it a first step. (*as they exit together*) I'm going on faith, here, Isaac. If this works, it's going to be quite a Father's Day gift.

ISAAC: Nothing but the best for you, Dad.

(*They exit.*)

THE GIFT

SYNOPSIS:
At the Bellini family reunion, grandmother and granddaughter share a token of faith that has been handed down through generations.

THEMES:
Faith
Family
Eternal life
Salvation

CHARACTERS:
Maxine (Bellini) Johannson, grandmother
Nicole Beckman, granddaughter

COSTUMES:
Maxine—summer skirt, top, and sandals
Nicole—T-shirt, shorts, and sandals or athletic shoes

PROPS:
Garbage sacks (2)
Lawn chairs (2)
Cross necklace
Maxine's reading glasses, on a chain around her neck

(Optional)
Banner—"Bellini Family Reunion"
Picnic table
Crumpled paper or plastic table covering
Plates, napkins, cups, etc.

SETTING:
Park, site of the Bellini family reunion

(MAXINE enters. She looks around in disgust and begins briskly picking up items and stuffing them into the garbage sack.)

MAXINE: What a mess! Who's going to clean this up? Me, I suppose.

(NICOLE enters with a soccer ball under her arm. She's passing through quickly but gets nabbed by her grandma.)

MAXINE: Hey, sweetie! Hold on a minute. What you are you doing?

NICOLE: Um—I'm just—

MAXINE: Do you have a second? Help your old grandma clean up. Just look at this place! This is the work of the shirttail relatives, I am sure. Family reunions are a lot of work.

(NICOLE glances over her shoulder somewhat regretfully, but she puts down the ball and joins her grandmother.)

NICOLE: Okay, Grandma. What do you want me to do first?

MAXINE: Why don't you gather up that trash? Here. *(She hands NICOLE a trash sack.)*

(NICOLE willingly gathers up trash as she finds it, but somewhat aimlessly.)

MAXINE: Look lively, dear. Your teens are passing you by.

(NICOLE speeds up. She, like all the other family members, is used to her grandmother's bossiness.)

Did you have a good time at the reunion, honey?

NICOLE: Yeah . . .

MAXINE: "Yes."

NICOLE: Yes. But Grandma. *(expressing a great discovery—)* Some of our relatives are *weird*.

MAXINE: A-men!

NICOLE: You're okay with that?

MAXINE: Family wouldn't be family if we didn't have a few colorful personalities thrown in for excitement. It keeps the reunions lively.

(*pointing*) Oops. Don't miss that one.

(*NICOLE puts the garbage in her bag.*)

NICOLE: Grandma? Are most of the people in our family Christians?

MAXINE: A lot of them are. It's something we handed down.

(*MAXINE indicates the two chairs and invites NICOLE to sit.*)

Your great-great-grandparents were believers in the old country, and when the family came to America, they brought their faith with them. And it has been passed on. My great-grandparents gave it to my grandparents, and they gave it to my parents, they gave it to me, Grandpa and I gave it to your mom, and she gave it to you. It's like a present.

NICOLE: I wonder what would have happened if someone along the way had decided not to be a Christian.

MAXINE: Well, everyone gets to choose, don't they? That's a choice. But we sure wouldn't be the same family.

NICOLE: I guess I'll be telling my kids about our family faith, too, someday. But—(*worried*) what if they don't believe me?

MAXINE: You'll do what I do. Pray and trust God. And give a little extra push now and then. Nothing wrong with that.

(*MAXINE stands again.*)

NICOLE: Like you do with Mom?

(*NICOLE stands.*)

MAXINE: Um . . . right.

NICOLE: Mom calls it nagging.

MAXINE: Oh, she does.

NICOLE: She says a grown woman can live her own life without a bossy busybody calling her up and—

MAXINE: (*clearing her throat and stopping NICOLE with a raised hand*) Your mother confuses persistent *persuasion* with nagging. But that's another story for another day.

NICOLE: I still wear the necklace, Grandma. (*showing necklace*) See?

MAXINE: (*adjusting glasses*) Yes, yes. Isn't it lovely? That cross was Great-Grandma's. All of us wore it as girls.

NICOLE: Mom gave it to me last year after I prayed and became a follower of Jesus.

MAXINE: Good. Don't ever forget the most important gift your family has given you.

NICOLE: The necklace?

MAXINE: No, no, your faith. It'll affect your whole life. I keep picturing the reunion we're going to have in heaven, someday.

NICOLE: I hope there's a game field. And a dessert table.

MAXINE: I hope there's a cleanup crew. Now, come with me, honey. Last I looked, the pavilion was just a mess. (*she starts to exit*) Are you still with me, Nicole?

NICOLE: (*following*) I'm with you, Grandma. (*She picks up the soccer ball.*)

(*They exit, MAXINE's arm around NICOLE, both carrying garbage bags.*)

One Tiny Disagreement

SYNOPSIS:
Coworkers share the bitterness and conflict that has developed between them. The unfolding dialogue demonstrates the inflexibility and lack of forgiveness that has made a situation spiral out of control. The drama is open-ended. Will the parties reconcile?

THEME:
Conflict
Bitterness
Forgiveness
Work situations
Inflexibility

CHARACTERS:
Larry, coworker
Stephen, coworker
Mindy, coworker
Jean, narrator

COSTUMES:
Larry, Stephen, and Mindy—modern work clothing
Jean—clothing that sets her apart from the others (black pants and shirt)

PROPS:
Chairs (4)

SETTING:
Office (but could be adjusted to another setting)

(Four chairs are arranged in a semicircle. There is a space between the two groups of two. All four characters enter. LARRY and STEPHEN sit on chairs to the right. MINDY sits on the outside chair to the left. JEAN stands behind her chair.)

JEAN: There was an intense disagreement between two groups of good people. Nobody exactly remembered how the problem started.

MINDY: What, are you kidding? I remember exactly how it started.

LARRY: Oh, let's not get into this again.

STEPHEN: Yeah, give it a rest!

(JEAN loses her calm demeanor and rolls her eyes in exasperation.)

JEAN: People, please—

MINDY: *(furious)* I have every right to be angry!

LARRY: What about us?

JEAN: STOP!

(Everyone freezes. After a moment, JEAN continues.)

It is true that there was fault on both sides. On one side *(she turns to LARRY and STEPHEN)* a lack of sensitivity to the needs of the other group. And on the other, inappropriate behavior in response.

STEPHEN: Inappropriate? That's what you'd call it? Inappropriate?

JEAN: *(exasperated)* All right. Unkind.

(STEPHEN and LARRY encourage further elaboration.)

Unattractive.

Un-Christian.

LARRY: Try unforgivable.

STEPHEN: (*to MINDY*) Some things *are* unforgivable, you know.

(*JEAN quickly sits down and puts her arms in front of the others to thwart a continuation of the verbal fight.*)

JEAN: So although the disagreement began small, it was fed with whispering, anger, and people taking sides, and it soon grew out of control.

STEPHEN: When people heard *our* side of things, they naturally aligned themselves with us.

LARRY: Rightly so.

MINDY: Plenty of people saw things *my* way.

JEAN: Although both groups had valid points, they had great difficulty seeing the other's side.

LARRY: (*indicating MINDY*) Well, come on. I mean—

JEAN: The good people established themselves as adversaries.

STEPHEN: People just don't heal after something like this. (*He looks significantly at MINDY, who looks away.*) Too many things have been said.

JEAN: The hostility grew. The bitterness escalated. Meetings turned into shouting matches. People stormed out in fury.

MINDY: (*under her breath*) There was a lot of juvenile behavior from their side.

STEPHEN: (*standing*) I've had enough of this!

(*JEAN gently pushes STEPHEN back into his chair.*)

JEAN: One day, the people again came together. Perhaps at this meeting they would have an opportunity to present their viewpoints to an openhearted audience. Perhaps they would even share forgiveness, resolve their disagreement and move forward with compassion—

(She pauses to look around at the group.)

or would just continue their bitterness and go their separate ways.

(Freeze. They exit.)

HOLDING PATTERN

SYNOPSIS:
Terese is in a hospital waiting room with her sister, Adele, and brother, Calvin. Her husband is in surgery, and things look grim. As they await an outcome, Terese talks about faith. She is not a believer and wonders what she has to cling to.

THEMES:
Life after death
Accidents
The unexpected
Family members who aren't believers
Bad news
Death
Preparing for death

CHARACTERS:
Terese, wife of Jake
Calvin, Terese's brother
Adele, Terese's sister

COSTUMES:
Terese, Calvin, and Adele—modern clothing

PROPS:
Chairs arranged as if in a waiting room
End tables
Magazines
Folded papers
Purse

(Optional)
Dividers to create a waiting area

SETTING:
Hospital waiting room

———————

(TERESE and CALVIN are sitting in chairs. TERESE's purse is on the floor or on the chair next to her. She is holding a magazine, but not reading it. CALVIN is visibly distracted and upset but silent. They're in a tense holding pattern, waiting for news. After a moment, ADELE rushes in. TERESE and CALVIN look relieved to see her and may murmur her name as they stand to embrace her.)

TERESE: You're here!

ADELE: I'm here, I'm here. *(She hugs TERESE for a long moment, then CALVIN.)* What's the news? Anything?

CALVIN: Almost nothing since we called. The surgeons said this first part would take the longest.

TERESE: I'm so glad you two are with me.

CALVIN: What are brothers for?

ADELE: And sisters?

(They all sit.)

CALVIN: I almost wish they'd come out and give us bad news, anything, just to end the suspense.

ADELE: *(outraged)* What are you yammering about, Calvin? *(Gesturing with her head and eyes toward TERESE.)*

CALVIN: *(hurriedly putting his hand on TERESE's)* I didn't mean that. We've just been waiting for all these hours—

TERESE: I can't take any more bad news . . .

ADELE: *(glaring at CALVIN)* Don't even think about that, Terese. *(mouthing angrily at CALVIN)* Cal-vin.

(CALVIN is embarrassed.)

CALVIN: I'm sorry. You know I love Jake. I don't want him to die—

(ADELE again glares at CALVIN who puts his head in his hands in resignation.)

TERESE: Adele, what if he dies? What if he dies?

ADELE: Let's not get ahead of ourselves. He has the best surgeons in the country. He's a young man.

TERESE: He's not ready. He was making lists of projects this morning, right up until they gave him the anesthetic . . . all the things he's been meaning to—

CALVIN: He'll get to the list. Of course he will.

TERESE: When the doctor talked to us, I just blocked out the statistics. *(She opens her purse and pulls out a folded packet of papers.)* They gave me this packet—"27 percent morbidity."

(She stands and moves toward a "door"—as if in the direction of the surgical suite.)

What if I've already said good-bye?

(CALVIN dejectedly hangs his head and ADELE miserably looks at her hands, both acknowledging this as true even though they don't want to.)

(suddenly turning to them) What do I do now?

(abruptly, upset) Don't just sit there!

ADELE: I don't know what to say.

TERESE: I know what you're thinking! Jake's going to be okay because of his faith, right? There's a God in heaven waiting for him. But what comfort is that to me? I don't believe any of that.

(*CALVIN tries to put his arm around her. She pulls away and moves back to look toward a "door," toward the surgery. She returns to look at them.*)

All these years I've thought all of you were just weak. Or misguided.

Now I wish I could believe like you do.

(*almost angry*) Can you give me any proof there's life after death? Or am I just supposed to trust?

How do I know for sure?

(*Freeze. Exit.*)

SMALL ACTS

SYNOPSIS:
In a coffee shop, Ellyn recognizes Grace, a woman who helped her escape an abusive relationship years ago by taking her and her children to a women's shelter. Grace's actions completely changed Ellyn's life.

THEMES:
Acts of kindness
Salt and light behavior
Acting like a Christian

CHARACTERS:
Grace
Ellyn

COSTUMES:
Grace and Ellyn—modern clothing

PROPS:
Coffee shop table
Chairs(2)
Newspaper
Styrofoam or paper coffee cups (2)

SETTING:
Coffee shop

(GRACE *enters, carefully carrying a full coffee cup with a folded newspaper under her arm. She takes a sip of her coffee to keep the cup from sloshing, then*

approaches the table and sits down. She opens the paper and starts to read, sip-
ping the coffee. ELLYN enters, also carrying coffee. As she passes Grace's
table, GRACE glances up and meets ELLYN'S eye. ELLYN stops.)

ELLYN: Grace?

GRACE: (*uncertainly, but pleasantly*) Yes?

ELLYN: Grace? I can't believe this! It's me! Ellyn! Ellyn Flynn. Don't
you remember?

GRACE: Yes. (*suddenly realizing*) Yes! Ellyn—you look so . . . different.
(*marveling*) Like a new person! (*She stands and embraces ELLYN.*)
It's great to see you! Can you join me?

ELLYN: I'd love to! (*She takes the other seat at the table.*)

GRACE: I'm surprised you remember me.

ELLYN: (*amazed*) Are you kidding? How could I forget? Grace, you saved
my life.

GRACE: (*laughing self-consciously*) I what?

ELLYN: You did.

GRACE: You're thinking of someone else!

ELLYN: (*growing serious*) I wouldn't have made it without you. Back
when we were neighbors, you were my lifeline.

GRACE: I hardly did anything. I prayed with you. And for you. But—

ELLYN: And bought us groceries. And drove my kids to school—

GRACE: It wasn't much. Just little things.

ELLYN: (*firmly*) You were always there. That was the hardest time of my
life, and you were the one, shining light when everything else

seemed hopeless. *(half laughing)* Is it too late to apologize? I leaned on you too much. I nearly smothered you. It's just that I needed someone so badly. I was desperate.

GRACE: Things were so bad for you. I wanted to do more.

What happened? I drove you and the kids to the women's shelter that night and then—I never heard from you again. Where did you go? I tried to find you.

ELLYN: I don't know why I didn't call you. I was embarrassed, or shell-shocked. I just wanted to start over and forget everything.

That night was the beginning of things turning around, even if it didn't feel like it at the time. The shelter helped me find a place for the kids and me. I got a job. I'm a teacher now. Fifth grade.

GRACE: That's what you wanted to do! What about the kids?

ELLYN: They're great. Beyond great. *(ELLYN pulls out her wallet and turns pages to a photograph that she shows to GRACE.)* Look. Gary. Martha. And this is the baby, Lisa.

GRACE: They're all grown up! Unbelievable.
This is an answer to prayer, running into you like this.

ELLYN: You did so much more than talk about being a Christian. You showed me. You took huge risks for me—for us. You put yourself in danger.

GRACE: I did little things.

ELLYN: But those little things made all the difference. *(She becomes emotional and can't go on.)*

(GRACE and ELLYN sit quietly for a moment, composing themselves.)

I keep wondering what would have happened without you, Grace. What would I have done? Where would I be now?

(Freeze. Exit.)

THE INSIDE STORY

SYNOPSIS:
Two women confront the temptations of everyday life. Each woman has a "twin" who stands behind her, sharing the way that she could turn a tempting scenario into a victory.

THEMES:
God's provisions
Honesty
Making hard, everyday decisions
Daily tests and choices
Holiness

CHARACTERS:
Her (narrator)
She (narrator)
Twin #1
Twin #2

COSTUMES:
Her and She—dressed identically, perhaps in denim shirts and khaki pants
Twin #1 and Twin #2—dressed identically in black pants and white shirts

PROPS:
None

SETTING:
None; the audience will imagine the setting as TWIN #1 and TWIN #2 mime situations

(TWIN #1 enters, turns toward the audience, and stops. After a moment, TWIN #2 enters and follows the exact same movements. HER and SHE enter and stand near the twins. During the drama, the narrators shadow the twins, using them as examples of the choices for good or evil. TWINS #1 and #2 simultaneously mime the situations while they are being described.)

(Scenario #1)

HER: You're late picking up the kids from school. You have exactly five minutes to get there.

SHE: You pull onto *(familiar local road)* and you're cruising. Your foot presses the accelerator.

HER: And then some guy pulls out in front of you. There's no one behind you for a mile, and yet this guy feels the need to roar out ahead of you.

SHE: In a split second, your decision is made . . .

HER: You make your message perfectly clear, accelerating and giving him a well-deserved scare by tailing dangerously close for a mile and a half.

SHE: You hit the brakes and give him room, asking God for patience and vowing to leave the house earlier tomorrow.

(Scenario #2)

SHE: The store is packed. And hot. You've been standing in line for twenty minutes. All you need are a couple of items.

HER: Two teenagers with an attitude start edging up next to you—

SHE: —pretending that they've been in line all along.

HER: You stand your ground, but they keep pushing ahead, jostling against you. Before long, they're ahead of you.

SHE: You can't believe the nerve. What you do next is priceless.

HER: You lash out, telling them how long you've been waiting and where the back of the line is. You feel great righteous satisfaction when everyone else turns to nod at you with approval and crossed arms.

SHE: You surprise yourself by speaking kindly to the girls and with warmth that actually comes from your heart.

(Scenario #3)
HER: This garage sale is amazing!

SHE: Among other deals, you find an old doctor's satchel for a few dollars. Obviously this family has no idea what they're selling.

HER: After you get home you open a compartment in the bag and find five twenty-dollar bills tucked inside. Your bargain just became a treasure.

SHE: You hold the bills in your hand, realizing that you have a choice. Keep the money as a reward for being such a skilled shopper.

HER: Or drive all the way back to the sale and quietly return the cash to the owners.

(Scenario #4)
HER: Monday night. The phone rings. It's been a long day at work, and you are exhausted.

SHE: Nancy again, calling for volunteers at church. What is it with this woman? She gets the prize for persistence, but is she totally dense? Doesn't she realize how busy you are?

HER: The kids are whining. The baby is crying.

SHE: There's homework to do and a whole week to survive.

HER: Do you really want to give up an hour every Sunday to teach fourth-graders about God?

SHE: Nancy's waiting . . .

HER: You explain for the third time how crazy life is right now. You tell her that you hope to do more ministry work in the future when you have some time, but it doesn't look like that's going to happen any time soon.

SHE: You find yourself wondering why Nancy thinks you would be a good teacher. What does she know that you don't know? You envision the students. You imagine sharing with them what you've learned about growing your faith. Suddenly you hear yourself telling Nancy to put you on the list.

(Conclusion)
HER: We face them every day.

TWIN #2: Little tests.

TWIN #1: Tiny choices.

SHE/HER: Significant opportunities for holiness.

(Freeze. Exit.)

THE SPEAKER

SYNOPSIS:
Karin suddenly leaves a lecture hall when it becomes clear to her that the instructor is not basing his information on well-founded research. She is confronted by Josie, who doesn't understand why Karin is so upset.

THEMES:
Evil teachers
False teachers
Discernment
Seeking truth

CHARACTERS:
Karin, a college student
Josie, her friend, also a college student

COSTUMES:
Karin and Josie—typical college-student clothing

PROPS:
Books
Notebooks
Backpacks

SETTING:
Outside a college lecture hall

(KARIN enters, carrying books and notebook, in a hurry. After a moment, JOSIE enters, following KARIN.)

JOSIE: Karin! Wait! Hold on! Where are you going?

KARIN: Back to the dorm.

(JOSIE catches KARIN's sleeve and stops her.)

JOSIE: You stormed out of the lecture hall like it was on fire. Are you sick or something?

KARIN: No, of course not. *(realizing)* Did I—just make a scene?

JOSIE: If you mean, "Did anyone notice as you climbed over chairs, bumping into everyone in the row and slamming the door so the room got deadly quiet and everyone felt awkward and uncomfortable?"—Yeah.

KARIN: The lecturer noticed, too?

JOSIE: Afraid so.

KARIN: I am so sorry. I just lost it. Suddenly I had to get out of there.

JOSIE: But why?

KARIN: Josie. Didn't you hear him?

(JOSIE holds out her palm in a "what?" gesture.)

The teacher. He was so off base.

JOSIE: Huh? He sounded pretty good to me.

KARIN: Hello! Were you even listening?

JOSIE: Yeah. I have pages of notes here.

KARIN: You wrote down what he said? Didn't any of it sound a little off to you?

JOSIE: Well—new, sure. Intriguing. Actually, he filled in a lot of gaps for me. Made me think.

KARIN: Maybe you should reread our texts from last semester. You might notice a few serious contradictions.

(*KARIN begins to exit.*)

JOSIE: (*calling after her*) Maybe you just aren't open to someone with new insights.

(*KARIN stops abruptly.*)

KARIN: But his "new insights" don't even build on any of the research that's been done to date. (*She holds up a textbook.*) Have you read this?

(*JOSIE shrugs a bit sheepishly, smiling.*)

KARIN: (*holding up another book*) This?

(*It's apparent she hasn't read either. KARIN places the books on top of JOSIE's load of books.*)

KARIN: Before rereading today's lecture notes, go back to 101. Read these.

JOSIE: (*taking another tack*) Why would he even be here if he didn't have something valid to say? He's gotten this far. He's earned a lot of acclaim. He's been published all over . . .

KARIN: Does that prove anything to you? You're not a sponge. We're supposed to be listening with our brains.

(*JOSIE, for the first time, looks uncomfortable.*)

KARIN: (*distracted, thinking out loud*) How does he get people to fall for this stuff? I mean, educated students.

(*KARIN looks at JOSIE in wonder.*)

KARIN: (*realizing*) They're all still in there.

(*Freeze. They exit.*)

A Small Story of Redemption

God has ways of engaging skeptical people in dialogue—through music, a pointed and personal sermon, dire difficulty, friendship. The Holy Spirit uses it all. God got me with theatre.

At the time, I was a peripheral Christian who had transferred from the practice of my faith to other worthy pursuits, namely creative writing and career. I was no longer interested in church. I had been disappointed, embittered. I was a believer, but not a follower, and I found it surprisingly easy to live outside of my beliefs (even while feeling twinges of sadness about losing proximity with God).

A friend invited me to write a script for a worship service at her church. She could have been truly desperate or perhaps misled, but she was a good friend and I said yes. It was an opportunity to write, something I rarely turn down.

I wrote a slice of life piece and sat uneasily in the back row of the sanctuary on the Sunday that it was presented. It went well enough. The piece intertwined with the rest of the service. People seemed engaged. I had to admit that the service wasn't what I had expected. The pastor was thoughtful, insightful even. He invited congregants into a relationship with God rather than a commitment to a political party. I was surprised, but not yet convinced. I hung around, waiting for the expected sound of the other shoe dropping.

I agreed to the next assignment, and the next. I was drawn into a community of actors, directors, and writers who were genuine, practicing Christians. A gradual evolution took place. During a series of rapid-fire crises, I felt peace—other-worldly peace—only when I was at worship. Drama had gotten me through the door, and the Holy Spirit had given a new start to a deadened, but not dead, faith. I fell in love.

I may be the only person in history to have renewed my faith because of worship drama, but my story shows that God can use a variety of unlikely tools to communicate good news.

Who knows who is sitting in the audience?